FUN FACT FILE: WORLD WONDERS!

20 FUN FACTS ABOUT THE GREAT WALL OF CHINA

By Therese Shea

Gareth Stevens
Publishing

Please visit our website, www.garethstevens.com. For a free color catalog of all our high-quality books, call toll free 1-800-542-2595 or fax 1-877-542-2596.

Library of Congress Cataloging-in-Publication Data

Shea, Therese.
20 fun facts about the Great Wall of China / by Therese Shea.
  p. cm. — (Fun fact file: world wonders!)
Includes index.
ISBN 978-1-4824-0475-3 (pbk.)
ISBN 978-1-4824-0476-0 (6-pack)
ISBN 978-1-4824-0472-2 (library binding)
1. Great Wall of China (China) — History — Juvenile literature. 2. Great Wall of China (China) — Design and construction — Juvenile literature. I. Shea, Therese. II. Title.
DS793.G67 S54 2014
931—dc23

First Edition

Published in 2014 by
Gareth Stevens Publishing
111 East 14th Street, Suite 349
New York, NY 10003

Designer: Sarah Liddell
Editor: Greg Roza

Photo credits: Cover, p. 1 Cavan Images/Stone/Getty Images; p. 5 Perkus/E+/Getty Images; p. 6 Grant Faint/Workbook Stock/Getty Images; p. 7 photo courtesy of Wikimedia Commons, EN-CHU260BCE.jpg; p. 8 Pan Hong/Flickr/Getty Images; p. 9 TEH ENG KOON/Staff/AFP/Getty Images; p. 10 Panorama Media/Getty Images; p. 11 forest_strider/Shutterstock.com; p. 12 Dorling Kindersley/Getty Images; pp. 13, 24, 29 Hung Chung Chih/Shutterstock.com; p. 14 Angus McBride/The Bridgeman Art Library/Getty Images; p. 15 © iStockphoto.com/lnzyx; p. 16 ChameleonsEye/Shutterstock.com; p. 17 Frank Lukasseck/Photographer's Choice/Getty Images; p. 18 EggHeadPhoto/Shutterstock.com; p. 19 Hanquan Chen/E+/Getty Images; p. 20 © iStockphoto.com/vincent369; p. 21 British Library/Robana/Contributor/Hulton Fine Art Collection/Getty Images; pp. 22–23 © iStockphoto.com/livetalent; p. 25 NASA NASA/Photo Researchers/Getty Images; p. 26 Louise Cukrov/Shutterstock.com; p. 27 MANDEL NGAN/Staff/AFP/Getty Images.

Printed in the United States of America

CPSIA compliance information: Batch #CW14GS: For further information contact Gareth Stevens, New York, New York at 1-800-542-2595.

Contents

Words in the glossary appear in **bold** type the first time they are used in the text.

Monument of Myth and History

An ancient Chinese story tells of a young man who was taken away from his wife and forced to help build the Great Wall of China. After hearing of his death, his wife cried so hard that part of the wall fell.

This is a well-known myth in China, but it also reveals some truths about the Great Wall. Many people were forced to build this **structure**, and many died while doing so. Amazingly, hundreds of years later, it remains standing—a lasting monument to the long, winding history of the Chinese people.

The Great Wall of China is one of the most well-known structures in the world because of its incredible length as well as its age.

A Long Wall with a Long History

FACT 1

The Chinese have a different name for the Great Wall.

Though the Western world calls the giant structure the Great Wall of China, the Chinese call it Wan Li Chang Cheng, or 10,000-Li-Long Wall. A *li* is a unit of measurement equal to about 1/3 of a mile (0.5 km).

The Chinese use characters when they write. This sign shows the characters they use for the Great Wall.

The Great Wall wasn't the first large wall in China.

At one point in China's history, there were many kingdoms at war with each other. The first kingdom we know of to build a defensive wall was called Chu. Soon, other kingdoms built walls for long-lasting **protection** from each other.

The Chu wall was called the Square Wall. This map shows the Chu kingdom around 260 BC.

7

FACT 3

Parts of the Great Wall of China are more than 2,200 years old.

The Chu wall dates as far back as the seventh century BC. Around 220 BC, **Emperor** Qin Shi Huang (CHIN SHEE HWAHNG) united several Chinese kingdoms. He ordered that walls be moved, connected, or built to create a structure thousands of miles long.

Qin Shi Huang was the first emperor of China. He wanted a wall built to protect China from enemies to the north, particularly a group called the Huns.

Parts of the Great Wall were repaired, destroyed, and extended.

The Great Wall of the Qin **dynasty** was altered many times.

The Great Wall we know today is mostly from the Ming dynasty.

During the 1400s, the Ming added land to their empire. For

greater protection, they created much of

the amazing structure we know today.

During the Ming dynasty, many structures were added to the Great Wall. These include temples, bridges, and towers.

FACT 5

Even today, the Great Wall isn't one continuous structure.

The Ming dynasty didn't just oversee the lengthening and widening of parts of the wall. They created **parallel** walls in some places, such as to the north of their capital city of Beijing. They did this to add more protection and confuse enemy forces.

Map of the Great Wall

Shenyang

Old Dragon's Head

Yanmenguan Pass

BEIJING

Yinchuan

Tianjin

Niangziguan Pass

Guguan Pass

Taiyuan

Pianguan Pass

Lanzhou

Zhenbeitai

Xian

FACT 6

People on both sides of the law built the Great Wall.

A wall of such size required a lot of workers. It's said that many kinds of people were used as manpower for the original wall—even criminals! A general named Meng Tian (MUHNG tee-UHN) oversaw construction and used his army as workers, too.

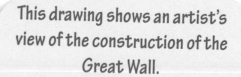

This drawing shows an artist's view of the construction of the Great Wall.

Sections of the wall built of earth didn't last as long as those made of stone.

FACT 7

The Great Wall is made out of many different kinds of materials.

Much of the wall is made of stone. However, stone wasn't always available. Workers sometimes used wooden tools to pack dirt tightly into wooden frames. Then, workers put the frames on top of that layer and packed more dirt. More layers were added until the wall reached the desired height.

Construction of the wall was more than just tough work—it was deadly.

The Great Wall earned the nickname the "longest **cemetery** on Earth" because so many people died while building it. Many sources **estimate** that over 1 million people died from causes such as terrible weather, deadly illnesses, lack of food, and unsafe work practices.

Many of the prisoners working on the wall were guilty of nonviolent crimes such as not paying taxes.

Many stories say that workers who died building the wall were buried in it.

Even though that's a popular tale, it's probably not true. No human remains have ever been found in the crumbling parts of the wall. However, Emperor Qin was said to have forced wives to take the place of their dead husbands at the wall!

Parts of the Great Wall are wide enough to drive a car on.

The Ming dynasty made parts of the wall very wide—about 22 feet (6.7 m) in some places. That was enough space for five soldiers on horseback to ride side by side. Invaders trying to tear down the wall had no chance.

FACT 11

Towers and fortresses were built atop the wall, giving it more height.

The Great Wall is more than a wall. Towers were built in the 1500s as posts for guards watching for enemy Mongols to the northwest. Larger **fortresses** were built near towns and other important sites that needed extra protection.

This fortress was restored in 1949. It's called the "Last Door Under Heaven." It marks the northwestern end of the Great Wall.

17

FACT 12

The wall was cleverly built for battle.

The Great Wall wasn't just a fence 24 feet (7.3 m) high.

Much of its eastern length was built for battle. The side facing

enemy territory was dotted with taller, rectangular sections

called *duokou*. Openings in each of these allowed soldiers to

keep watch and shoot arrows.

duokou

Some enemies tried to climb the wall with ladders, but guards on duty could often stop them.

The Great Wall of China by the Numbers

approximate length: 5,500 miles (8,850 km)

average width at the base: 24.5 feet (7.5 m)

average width at the top: 19 feet (5.8 m)

number of watchtowers: more than 25,000

average height: 24.5 feet (7.5 m)

FACT 13

Messages sent along the wall could travel more than 600 miles (965 km) in a day!

Regular signal towers along the wall allowed soldiers to spread news quickly. Smoke signals were used during the day. Fires were used at night. Soldiers on the front lines could warn leaders of an approaching enemy or report a victory.

Smoke signals and fires sent messages faster than a rider on horseback.

The Great Wall couldn't stop a major invasion in the 1600s.

You might think the wall would stop any enemy. That's not true. Invaders from Manchu to the northeast found a way through the wall in 1644. How? A **rebel** general opened the gate at Beijing and let them in! That was the end of the Ming dynasty.

Work on the Great Wall stopped after the Manchu invasion. The wall continued being a roadway for soldiers and a way for people to send important messages, though.

FACT 15

Until recently, people weren't sure how long the Great Wall is.

The length of the wall has been questioned for many years.

Estimates ranged from 1,500 miles (2,414 km) to about

4,000 miles (6,437 km) long. Because the wall passed through

mountains, deserts, and other landforms hard to

explore, it was tough to measure.

The Great Wall is longer than the distance between New York City and Athens, Greece.

A study in 2009 revealed that the Great Wall is about 5,500 miles (8,850 km) long. This includes land formations that were considered part of the wall, such as wide rivers, narrow hills, and tall mountains. These were just as hard to cross as the man-made wall.

About 70 percent of the Great Wall of China is man-made. It's the largest man-made structure in the world!

This section of the Great Wall ends in a lake.

FACT 17

One part of the Great Wall wasn't discovered until 2009.

The study of the Great Wall's length revealed about 180 miles (290 km) of wall that had been buried by sand or hidden by hills and rivers. Some of the sections couldn't have been found without tools such as **GPS**.

Disappearing Treasure

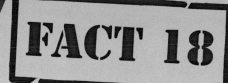

FACT 18

As much as half of the Great Wall isn't there anymore.

After the Manchu invasion, the wall wasn't cared for. About 50 percent of the wall has disappeared since then. In many places, it grew weak and fell apart because of earthquakes, harsh weather conditions, and plant overgrowth. Battles also damaged it.

Great Wall

People have said the Great Wall can be seen from space. While that's not true, it can be seen clearly in satellite images like this.

FACT 19

The Great Wall is still in danger of disappearing.

The greatest danger to the remaining wall is **tourism**. People exploring the wall cause harm even without meaning to. Some people write and paint on the stones and even take pieces home with them. The Chinese government now has laws limiting activities on the wall.

In 2009, President Barack Obama visited a section of the Great Wall near Badaling, China.

FACT 20

About 10 million tourists visit the Great Wall each year, including many famous people.

Millions of people visit the Great Wall each year. It's an important part of the Chinese economy. Barack Obama, Alicia Keys, Beyoncé, and Jaden Smith are just some of the people you might know who have visited the Great Wall.

Preserving Greatness

The Great Wall of China was named a World **Heritage** Site by UNESCO (United Nations Educational Scientific and Cultural Organization). This means the structure has great value not only for its length and size but also for its role in world history.

Hopefully, the World Heritage Site recognition will lead to more efforts to preserve, or save, the Great Wall. After more than 2,500 years, such a remarkable feat of human strength and resourcefulness shouldn't be allowed to crumble.

The China Great Wall Society and the International Friends of the Great Wall are working to preserve the famous structure.

29

Glossary

cemetery: an area where the dead are buried

dynasty: a line of rulers from the same family

emperor: a man who rules an empire

estimate: to make a careful guess about an answer based on the known facts

fortress: a protected place for the military

GPS: stands for "global positioning system." It uses satellites to find objects and places on Earth.

heritage: something handed down from the past

parallel: running in the same direction but not crossing

protection: the act of guarding

rebel: one who fights to overthrow a government

satellite: an object that circles Earth in order to collect and send information or aid in communication

structure: something that has been built, such as a building or monument

tourism: the business of drawing in tourists, or people traveling to visit a place

For More Information

Books

Coupe, Robert. *The Great Wall of China*. New York, NY: PowerKids Press, 2013.

Henzel, Cynthia Kennedy. *Great Wall of China*. Edina, MN: ABDO, 2011.

Roberts, Russell. *Ancient China*. Hockessin, DE: Mitchell Lane, 2013.

Websites

The Great Wall
travel.nationalgeographic.com/travel/world-heritage/great-wall-china
Read more about the Great Wall and other World Heritage sites.

How the Great Wall of China Works
www.howstuffworks.com/great-wall-of-china.htm
Find out more about the Great Wall from its beginning to present day.

Index